MAKING
GOURD ORNAMENTS
FOR *Holiday Decorating*

Angela Mohr

4880 Lower Valley Road Atglen, Pennsylvania 19310

DEDICATION

To my husband, David Lasko, who kindly turns a blind eye to all the gourds sitting around the house, who continues to park his car at the curb because of all the gourds and gourd projects filling the garage, and who has been known to buy an extra shed for gourd storage in the backyard. Truly, David is a saint on earth and I am blessed for having him in my life.

CONTENTS

Other Schiffer Books on Related Subjects
*Creating Christmas Ornaments from Polyme*r Clay,
0-88740-850-8, $12.95
Carving Seasonal Decorations,
0-7643-0715-0, $14.95

Copyright © 2007 by Schiffer Publishing, Ltd.
Library of Congress Control Number: 2007931190

Designed by Mark David Bowyer
Type set in AlgerianD / Zurich BT

ISBN: 978-0-7643-2716-2
Printed in China

Published by Schiffer Publishing Ltd.
4880 Lower Valley Road
Atglen, PA 19310
Phone: (610) 593-1777; Fax: (610) 593-2002
E-mail: Info@schifferbooks.com

For the largest selection of fine reference books on this and related subjects, please visit our web site at
www.schifferbooks.com
We are always looking for people to write books on new and related subjects. If you have an idea for a book please contact us at the above address.

This book may be purchased from the publisher.
Include $3.95 for shipping.
Please try your bookstore first.
You may write for a free catalog.

In Europe, Schiffer books are distributed by
Bushwood Books
6 Marksbury Ave.
Kew Gardens
Surrey TW9 4JF England
Phone: 44 (0) 20 8392-8585; Fax: 44 (0) 20 8392-9876
E-mail: info@bushwoodbooks.co.uk
Website: www.bushwoodbooks.co.uk
Free postage in the U.K., Europe; air mail at cost.

WHY GOURDS?

Gourds? Yes! Gourds can be made into holiday ornaments! Hard-shelled gourds, the inedible part of the squash family, have been used for thousands of years to make all manner of useful and decorative items for the home. Unlike the edible squashes, hard-shelled gourds will dehydrate and then have hard, woody walls. Many gourds have been referred to through the years by their functions: dipper gourds, canteen gourds, and powder horn gourds. Other gourds have been named to reflect their distinctive shape: apple gourds, snake gourds, and bottleneck or birdhouse gourds.

Gourds grow on vines that resemble pumpkin plants and can take over a trellis, fence, or garden space with dense growth. The developing gourds are green, sometimes mottled with light and dark green stripes, and are mostly water weight. When harvested and left to dehydrate, they turn brown or tan, still have their shape, are light for their size, and rattle with seeds when shaken. The dried molds and peeling skin on a dehydrated gourd can confuse folks into thinking they have rotted. Many a good gourd has seen the dump because it was thought to have rotted! But no, just soak it in warm water for a little while, clean off the surface debris with a scrubbie used for metal pots, and it's ready to accept all manner of art media.

TURNING GOURDS INTO ORNAMENTS

Almost any miniature gourd can be crafted into an ornament. With a bit of wire, some paint, and imagination, even scraps of large gourds can be made into dangling ornaments of beauty and fun. For the projects in this book, we will be using miniature bottleneck gourds (also called birdhouse gourds). They have the distinctive hourglass shape that works well for our purposes.

Miniature gourds have not been plucked from the vine early to retain their small size. They are fully mature gourds, grown the entire season, harvested, and dehydrated by passing breezes just like the full-sized gourds. All the dehydrating surface dirt and debris has been cleaned away with a metal pot scrubbie and warm water so the it's smooth and ready for some artistry. Throughout the pages of this book, you will see broad variations in gourd sizes and, sometimes, slight differences in their shape. Keep in mind that a gourd is a product of nature and as a result has all the interest and glory of the vast outdoors with undulating forces of cross pollination, weather, and ground minerals. Every gourd is an exercise in flexibility! A lesson for life in general, right?

These two gourds look similar and are referred to as bottleneck or birdhouse gourds; the little one is a miniature version of the larger one. Both are fully mature and ready to be used in a project.

These are all from the same type of plant in the same part of the garden. Nature produces a wide variation in finished products!

Part 1:

FIGURING OUT THE HANGING PART

The most simple, and probably the oldest, way to hang a gourd is with its own stem if it has retained enough curve from the growing process. Not all gourds were lucky enough to dance with nature in that way, so the next easiest hanging device is the screw-in eyehook, which often are packaged in sets of 12 and can be found in hardware stores. Bore a small hole into the gourd, add a dot of wood glue, and screw the eyehook into the hole. Give the glue time to dry. The glue wraps around the threads of the screw and, after it's dried, the threads act as a grip to keep the eyehook from becoming loose.

Another personal touch I like to add to my ornaments is a specially prepared ornament hook. It adds a finished look to an ornament and is worth the effort when I have a little extra time. I will review the wire curling technique to make these hooks. You may want to make sets of hooks for all your ornaments, or make sets of hooks as gifts!

But first, let's make some hanging devices.

Eyehooks can be screwed into the stem area of the gourd. There are various sizes of eyehooks available, these are .5" and found in many local hardware shops.

Here are some gourds with stems naturally formed into hook shapes. They hang fairly well, and if you're decorating with a nature theme, they would be perfect!

As a personal touch, I make my own hanging devices for ornaments because I like choosing wire that matches the look of the gourd ornament I am making. Packages of wire come in copper, steel, black steel, and brass. I will be showing you three hanging devices in this book: a Wrap, a Double Loop, and a Ring.

A Wrap

A Wrap is made by cutting one piece of wire and wrapping it around an existing stem. Before attempting this hanging technique, check to see if your stem is sturdy. A weak stem will break and ruin your efforts.

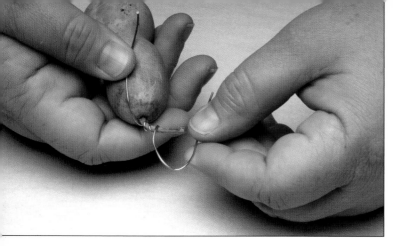

Hold one end of a 10" or longer wire against the gourd with about 2-3" under your thumb and wind the longer end of the wire around the stem until you reach a spot where, when hanging, the gourd will be balanced.

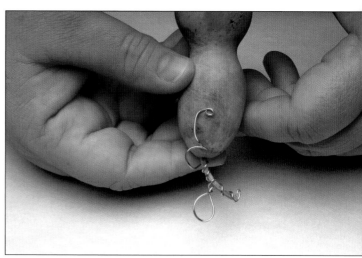

Elongate the wire a little and curl the end to avoid leaving a sharp edge.

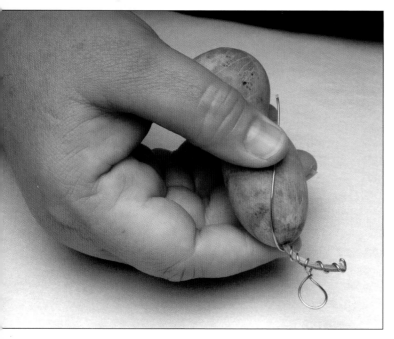

Twist a loop in the wire at the 'balance point', and continue wrapping until the wire is spent. Curl the end of the wire to avoid leaving a sharp edge.

The finished Wrap hanger

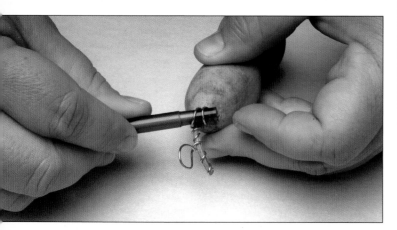

Go back to the original end of the wire under your thumb. Wrap this end around a pencil or pen to get a spiral.

A Double Loop

The Double Loop is a subtle hanger and worth the extra effort when you want a delicate looking, yet strong loop to hang your ornament. It is also the hanger to use if you like the eyehook look, but want a different color wire. The size of the Double Loop is dependent on what you wrap the wire around. Small ornaments will need smaller loops than larger ornaments. Remember, a gourd is a natural product and each one will be individual so *be* like a gourd, be *flexible*!

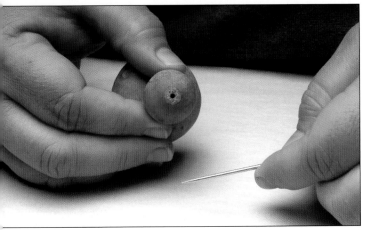

Using a darning needle, or other drilling tool, make a hole into a gourd where the stem end was at one time.

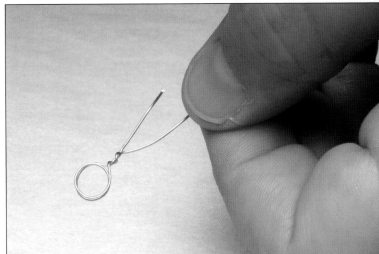

Wrap the wire around some kind of cylinder twice, letting the ends cross naturally…

Cut a piece of wire about 3-4" in length.

And twist twice. This twisting forms the threads the glue will grip as it dries.

Squeeze wood glue into the hole made in the gourd and insert the two ends into the hole and gently push the double loops toward the hole until the wire ends are inside the gourd and the loops nestle next to the hole. Let dry.

A Ring

The Ring is basically a large circle with ends that insert into a hole on opposite sides of a gourd. This is a versatile hanging device that can be personalized easily. Using a bit of imagination, you can crimp the sides of the wire, or twist spirals, or thread it with beads. How much wire you use depends on the size of the circle needed to reach from the hole on one side of the gourd and over the top to the hole on the other side of the gourd.

Using a darning needle or small drill bit, bore a hole into opposite sides of a gourd.

Cut a piece of wire and wrap it around a cylinder to get a circle.

Insert one end of the Ring into a hole on one side of the gourd, and the other end of the Ring into the opposite hole. Compress the circle ends into the gourd, so you can imagine they are probably overlapping inside the gourd.

The finished Double Loop hanger

The finished Ring hanger

Variations on the Ring can give a personalized touch to different ornaments.

Ornament Hooks

Ornaments hooks are nothing more than twisted bits of wire used to hang an ornament on a tree. Specialty wires of copper, brass, or steel add interest and can become part of the design by making the hook a permanent part of the ornament. However, for demonstration purposes, I will be using my favorite wires – the packages of pre-bent hooks bought at my local Wal-Mart. They are easy to find, consistent in size, and inexpensive. You can't go wrong with them.

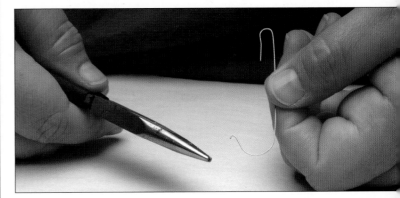

Using a pair of needle-nose pliers, pinch the very tip of the large end of a hook and bend it backwards.

Collapse the bent part so it folds back on itself.

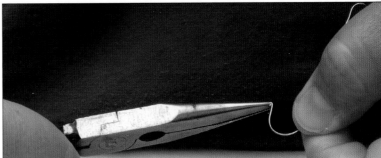

Pinch this collapsed part in the very end of the pliers and, holding the pliers still, use your free hand to bend the hook wire around the collapsed part to start making a coil.

Reposition the pliers and bend more wire around the collapsed part continuing the coil.

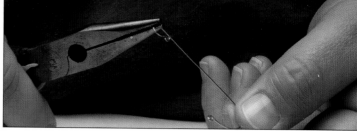

Use the needle-nose pliers to round out the hooking part if needed.

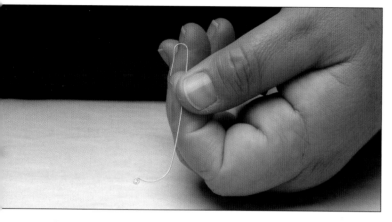

Place the coiled part in the flat area of the pliers and give it a good squeeze to flatten out any twists. The wire should be tightly coiled against itself with no gaps.

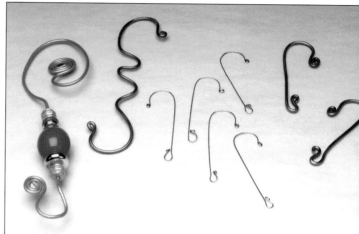

Finished ornament hooks made from a variety of wires. I even like to buy lengths of electrical conduit, which has seven pieces of copper twined together. I separate the pieces of copper and use them individually to make these hooks big enough to hang wreaths and bows on the front door. Throwing beads on them before curling adds a festive touch.

Use the needle-nose pliers to round out the hooking part if needed.

Opposite Page:
From left to right: Miniature bottleneck gourds (either grow them, buy them locally, or order them online from a gourd farm); fat darning needle and a drill bit to make holes (tie a bright ribbon through the needle's eye or around the first thread of the bit so you don't lose it in the shuffle of having fun); a woodburning tool (I buy these in the craft aisle at Wal-Mart—inexpensive enough that I keep two on hand: one with a rounded tip and one with a chisel tip); wood glue; a variety of wires (prepackaged 18 or 20 gauge steel or copper from the hardware aisle; I used 24 gauge brass jewelry wire from the craft aisle for the Angels and a piece of electrical conduit wire as a temporary wire for the Snowman project); Needle-nosed pliers; bits of ribbon; a variety of permanent markers. Permanent markers now come in a wide range of colors that makes coloring small details easy. (Again, nothing expensive—I bought mine at Wal-Mart in the school supplies aisle); a package of pre-bent ornament hooks; a little bottle of black craft paint; a can of glossy white spray paint; a can of metallic spray paint; round or square toothpicks; thin branches from yard bushes; grocery marker (this is a fat permanent marker found in the office supply aisle and I use it to wrap wire around—a 1" dowel or little craft paint bottle would do as well); spray lacquer or some other sealant (this adds shine and protects the gourd—always go lightly in several coats because permanent markers, though handy, can bleed a little if hit with a thick layer of sealant all at once); sandpaper (I use Sandblaster sandpaper because it is non-clogging and colored—the color I like because it helps me find it among the jumble on the workbench, a plus in my life).

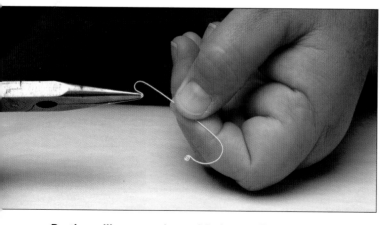

Do the coiling procedure with the smaller end of the hook.

Part 2:

THE RIGHT STUFF
FOR MAKING ORNAMENTS

Now, a word or two about equipment and what is needed to make interesting and gourdeous ornaments. There are gourd artisans I admire greatly who use pieces of equipment I can only aspire to, but will probably never own. Their end products show a level of detail and precision that reflect the quality of their tools and their patience. In general, you can find a full range of prices and quality through local and online sources. Depending on your personal art style and motives, the costs of equipment and supplies can be adjusted to fit your budget needs.

I personally use what I have on hand in the house or in the garage. Sometimes I will need a tool to do a specific job and that need will inspire me to make a tool out of, or make adjustments to, what I already own. I buy everything I use at my local Wal-Mart or

Ace Hardware shop. I have no pretensions; I'm a gourdhead more interested in having fun than accumulating tools I would be afraid to use for fear of breaking something. I do *a lot* of experimenting in the garage and if I ruin a $5 tool, no biggie. If I ruin a $50 tool, my heart is breaking.

This is what I used to make the gourd ornaments in this book. I included some comments to help you make substitutions. You may also have tools already on hand that I have never seen! Flexibility is the order of the day and if you can make something you already own work, then by all means do!

See? You probably already have most of this on hand or can make substitutions, so let's get started!

LET'S MAKE SOME ORNAMENTS!

Birdhouse

Using a drill bit, slowly turn a hole into the gourd, centering it top-to-bottom on the bottom bulge of the hourglass shape. A drill will make short work if you are making many ornaments, but holding a drill bit and gently turning it will work as well.

Select a miniature bottleneck gourd with a recognizable birdhouse hourglass shape. Check to see that at least one side is free from flaws or dark spots so that the front of the birdhouse will be clear for words and art.

Empty the seeds and any loose pith that may be rattling inside the gourd. Seeds and small debris will shake out; larger pieces can be pulled out with tweezers.

Using a woodburning tool with a rounded tip, write "Welcome Home" over the hole.

Using a woodburning tool with a chisel tip, burn a vine shape on either side of the hole.

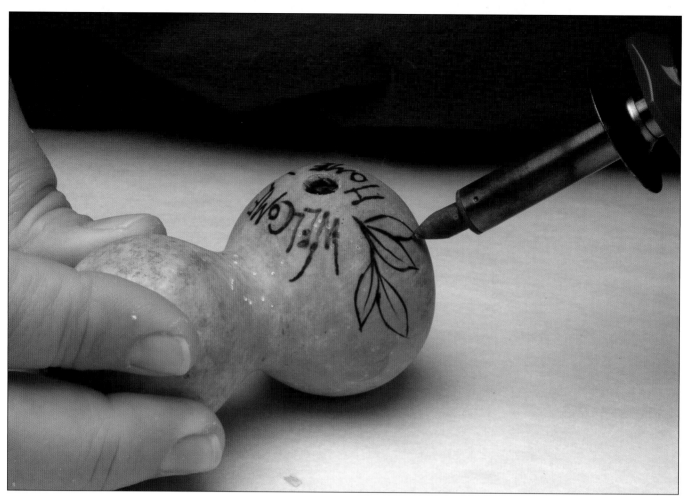

Add leaves to the vine by making pointed ovals at irregular intervals.

Color the leaves with permanent markers. Alternating two colors of green will add visual interest.

Holding the gourd with the birdhouse hole facing you, place eyeball points on opposite sides of the top bulge that will be used for the hanging device.

Bore holes on opposite sides of the gourd using a large darning needle.

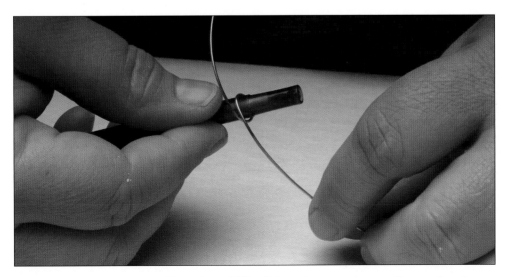

Cut about 5 inches of wire. Wind the middle of the wire around a pencil to make a loop.

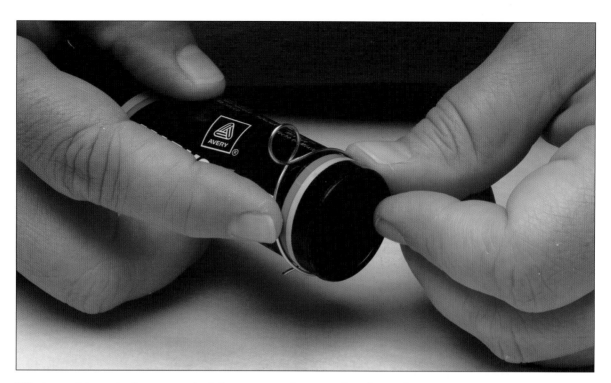

Wind remaining wire legs around a fat grocery marker to make a large ring.

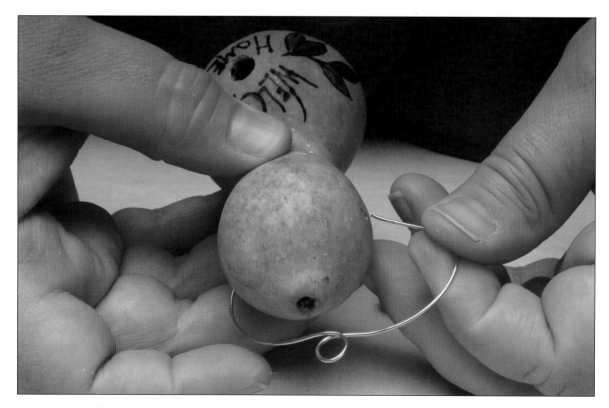

Insert ends of the large ring into the hanging holes.

Suspend ornament and spray lightly with lacquer or brush on a thin coat of polyurethane. Let dry and apply a second coating.

Snowman

Reviewing your stash of bottleneck gourds, select one that resembles a snowman. Make sure it has a smooth side, free from flaws. We are making only one snowman, but for future knowledge, it takes almost the same amount of time to make several snowmen as it does to make one. So doing more might be better.

When the gourd is thoroughly dry, lay it down so the front is facing up. (The gourd stays suspended on the temporary wire.)

On the top bulge of the gourd, about the place where ears would exist, use a scrap piece of conduit as a temporary wire and go into one side and continue out the other side so the gourd is suspended. The cut edge of your temporary wire will be rough enough to twist and make the holes.

Spray with white paint. Depending on the brand of paint you use, a second coat may be needed.

Using an orange permanent marker, color an end of a round or square toothpick. Cut off the colored end of the toothpick to make a carrot nose for the snowman.

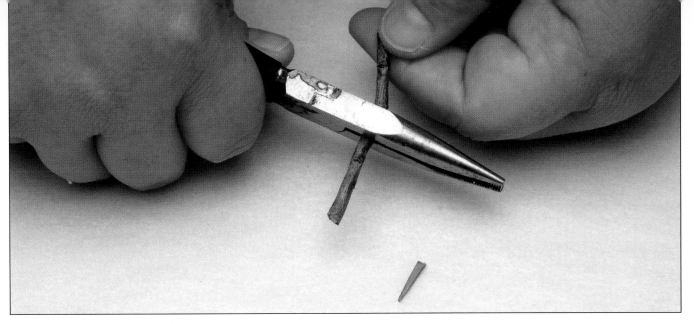

Trim two small branches for the arms. Note: Branches with bends or curves are more interesting than straight sticks.

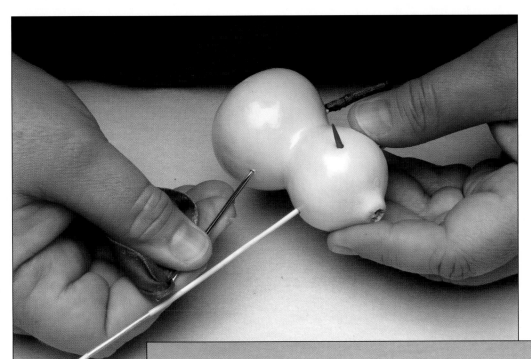

Using a darning needle, make holes in the gourd big enough to fit the toothpick carrot into the nose area and the branch pieces into the arm areas. Test the pieces to make sure they fit snugly, but are not difficult to insert.

Squeeze wood glue into the hole for the nose and insert the orange toothpick, blunt end first, so that the pointy end is sticking out looking like a carrot nose.

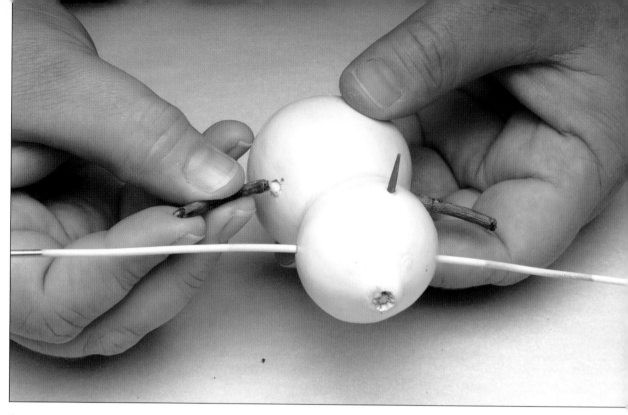

Squeeze wood glue into the holes for the arms and insert the branches.

Dot black craft paint onto the gourd where the coal eyes, mouth, and buttons should be. Let everything dry thoroughly.

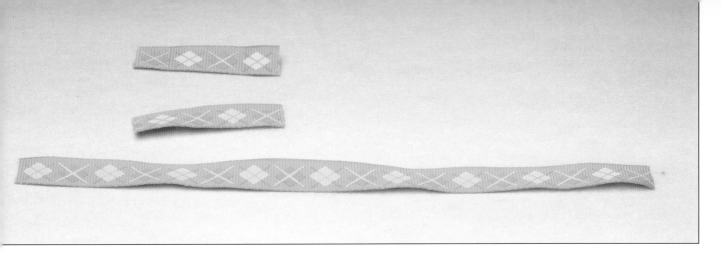

Select a length of ribbon to be used for the scarf and earmuffs; 12 inches should be enough. Cut one 9-inch piece and two 1.5 inch pieces. Note: The 9-inch piece will be longer than you need, but that will make tying the scarf easier. You can trim the excess away afterward.

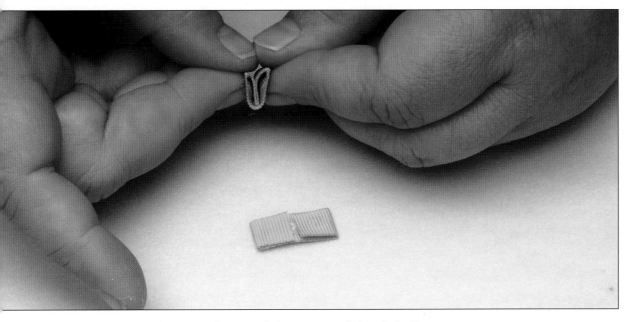

Fold each 1.5" piece as shown: ends toward the center and then in half.

Use a darning needle to puncture a hole through the earmuff ribbon layers. Move the folded ribbon up the needle to the fatter end so a hole is stretched into the ribbon. Leave for now.

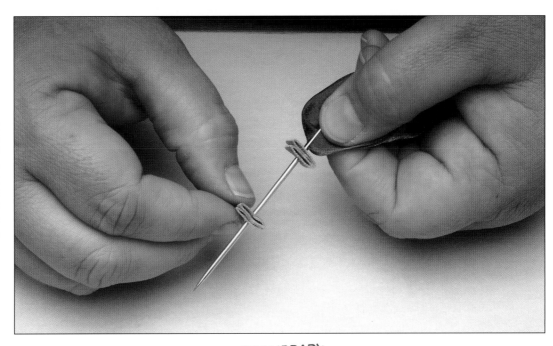

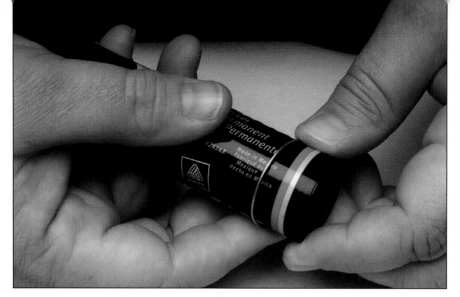

Cut a piece of wire and shape it into a ring by wrapping it around a fat grocery marker.

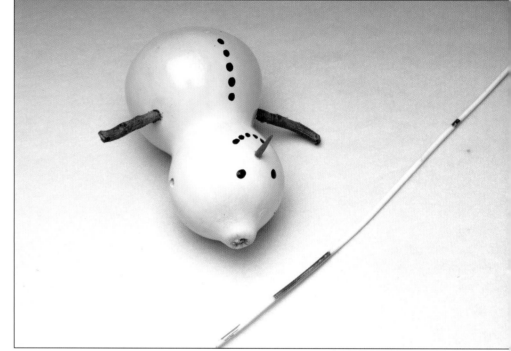

(When thoroughly dry,) remove the snowman from the temporary wire.

Without letting the folded ribbons pop open, remove the darning needle from one folded ribbon and thread onto one end of the wire ring. The hole left by the darning needle should be big enough to fit the wire.

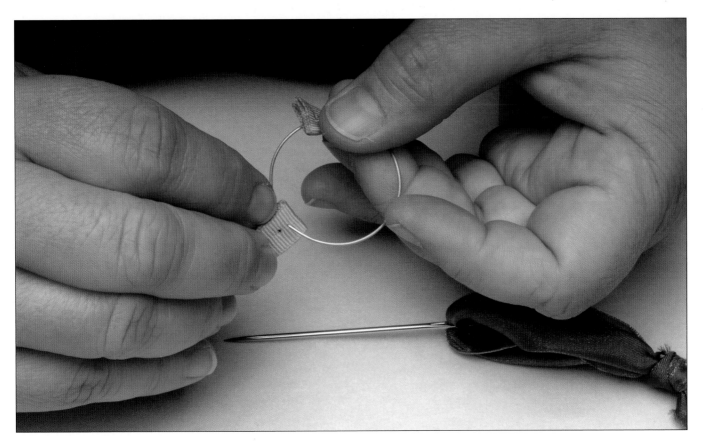

Repeat this step with the other folded ribbon for placement at the other end of the wire ring.

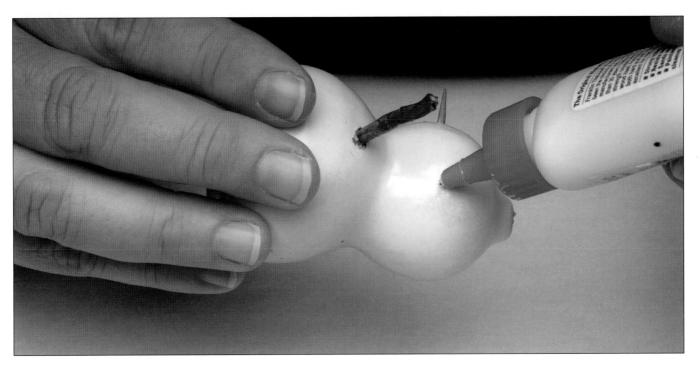

Dot the gourd's ear holes with wood glue.

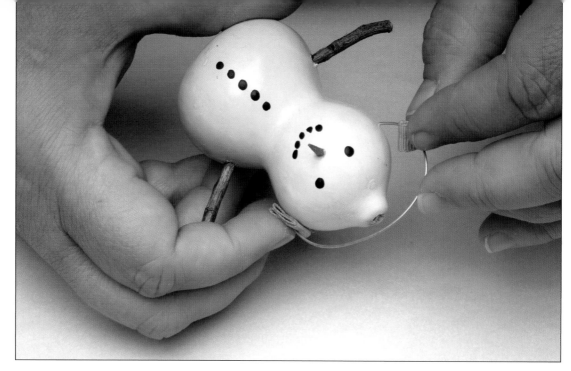

Fit the ends of the wire ring with the folded ribbon into the ear holes and press the wire into the gourd until you get a desirable 'earmuffs' look. The wire will hold the ribbons in place. Reshape the ring if need be.

Tie the 9" piece of frayed ribbon around the neck in a scarf-like fashion. If it keeps popping up, as some ribbons will, dot the underside with a smidgeon of glue and hold down with a pin until dry.

Angel

This ornament uses a technique of repetitive lines called "shadowing". When we use shadowing on the Angel's hair and garb, we will be placing three or four lines at irregular intervals around the gourd as a guide for the rest of the lines. Then by repeating the lines over and over and over, the 'hairs' or the fabric folds are shadowed. No lines will be perfect or straight, or evenly spaced for that matter...and they shouldn't be. The uneven spacing between the lines is what makes this technique work. As long as you have a broad idea of the hairdo you want to make, or the flow of the skirt, just keep adding lines to suit your tastes.

Turn the gourd upside-down since the tapering stem end will be the bottom of the Angel. Remove any stem pieces that may still be attached.

Select a gourd with an hourglass shape and a tapering stem end. For this ornament, a smooth, flaw-free gourd would be optimal since there will be art around the whole gourd.

Using a woodburner with a rounded tip, judge where the eyes would probably be on the top bulge and burn two lines for closed eyes and add three or four slanting eyelash lines to each line.

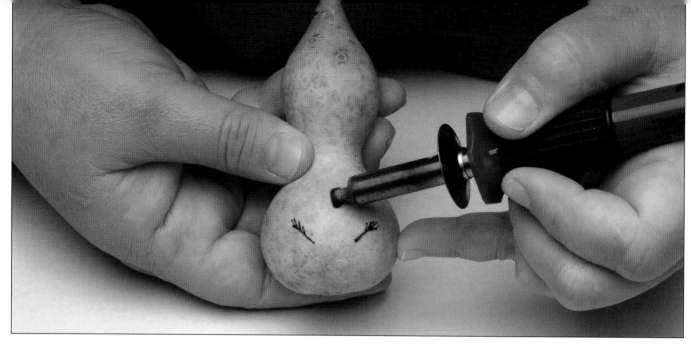

Below the closed eyes, burn an oval shape in the center (about the place where a mouth would be) for a singing mouth.

Below the curve of the gourd, burn a neckline that continues at least one-third to one-half the distance around the neck area. Add lines to imply gathers in the fabric or trim.

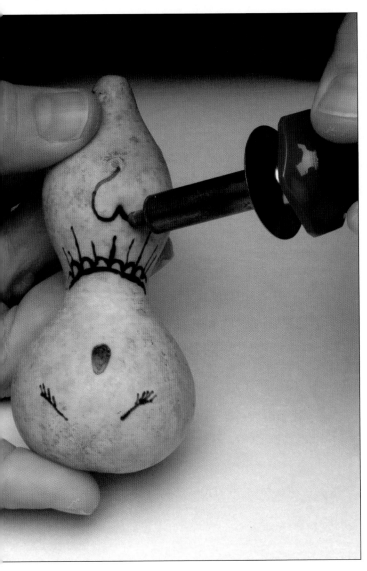

On the belly of the lower bulge, burn a heart shape. This will be the center point where the arms come together eventually.

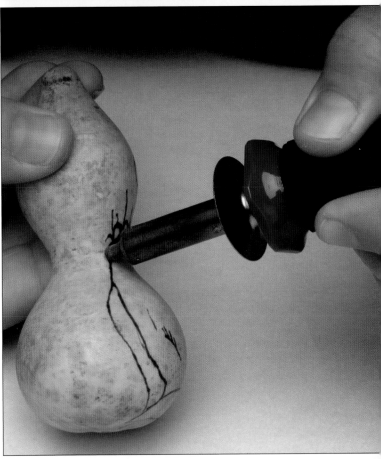

In this angel, we will create a long curly hairdo. Burn the basic outline of where the hair will go in front and sides…

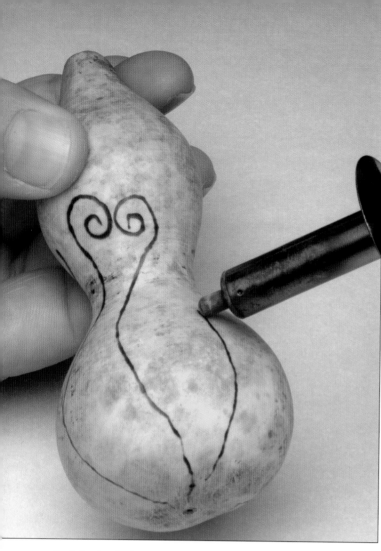

And the back. Remember we are creating a long curly hairdo on this angel so make the lines a little wavy and with some curl at the ends.

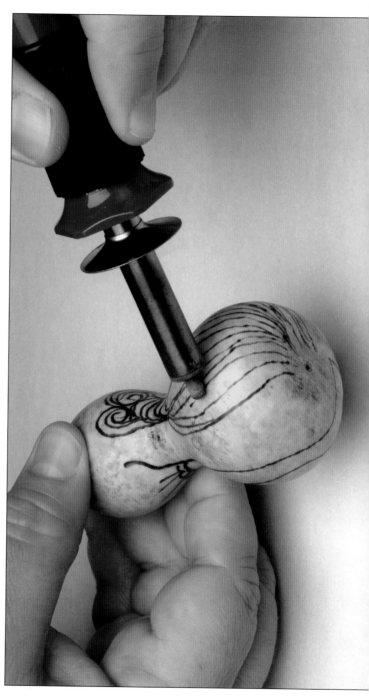

More and more lines, adding some variations among the lines—hair is never perfect!

Keep adding lines to mimic the original lines. Let's start on the back since we are already there.

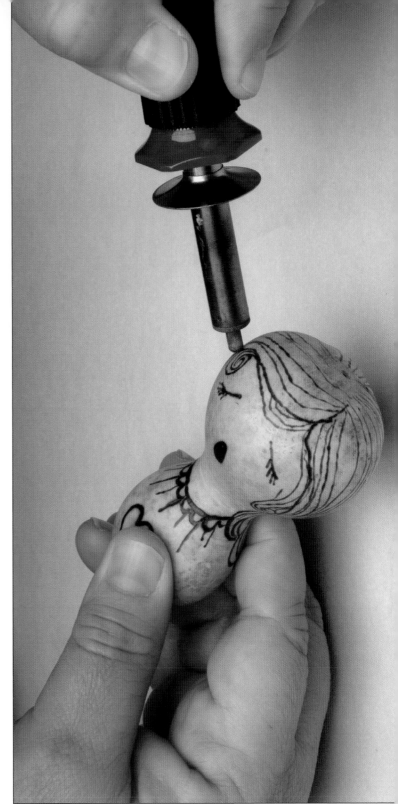

And then the front. You can keep adding curls and lines until you are happy with the hairdo. Make sure some hair lines meet the neckline edges so it looks like the hair is falling over the neckline of the shift she is wearing.

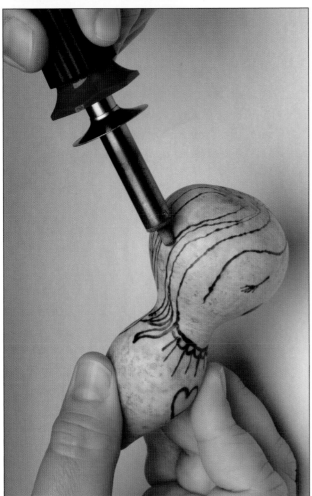

Move on to one side, and the other side…

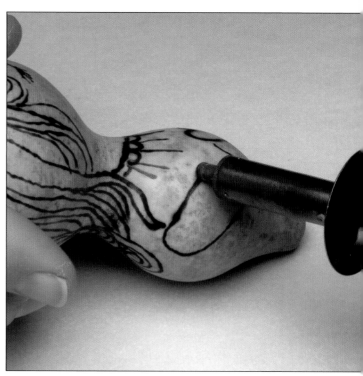

And then the other side. Notice that we took the arm lines from the long hair on the other side toward the heart as if the hair is covering the top part of the arm. On this side, we burned the hair lines swept away a little so that the shoulder is showing.

Add arms by burning parallel lines that come from the side of the gourd toward the heart, making the lines at the sleeve wider than the lines at the shoulder. Add fringe or scallops at the hem. First, one side...

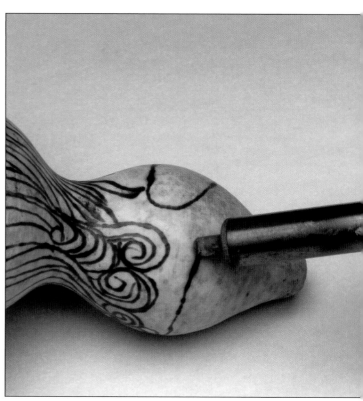

Burn a waistband around the center of the bottom bulge that goes from one elbow area to the other elbow area.

Burn lines from the waistband down toward the tapering end in the shadowing technique used for the hair, though with not as many lines. I will start under this arm since I am already there.

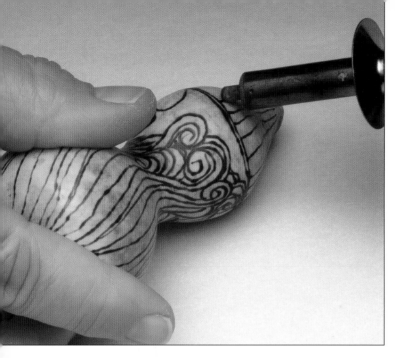

And continue around the back…

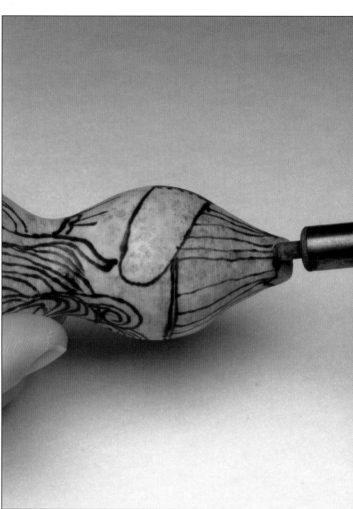

Burn a line around the tapering end to connect all the skirt's lines.

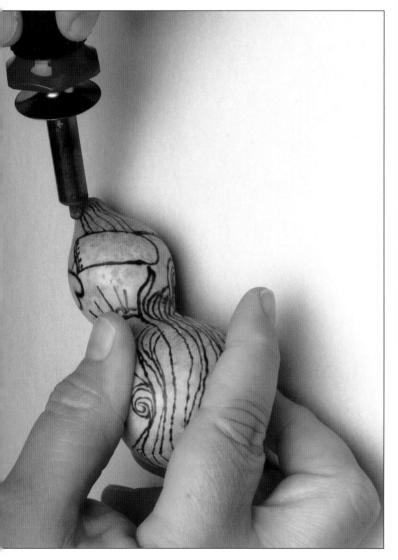

And onto the other side and front. Details to fabric are a personal choice. (When I have time, I like to add dots or other designs to the skirt.)

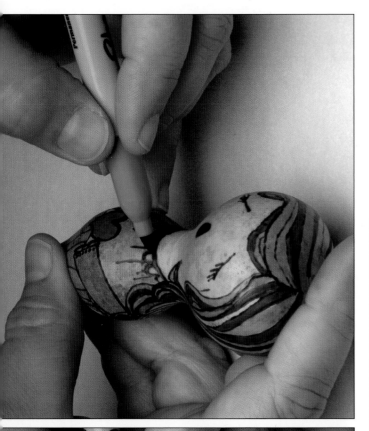

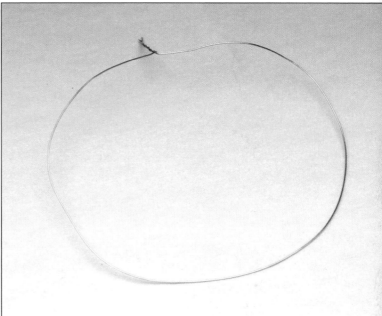

To make wings, cut a piece of 24 gauge brass wire to a length of about 12 inches and twist the ends together. You have a rough circle.

Color the gourd with permanent markers as shown here on the front and the back.

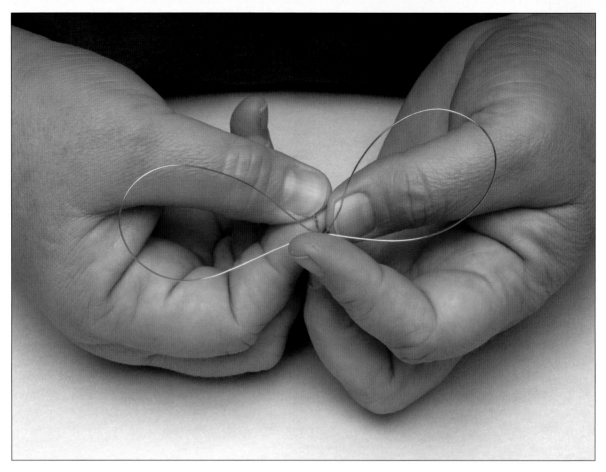

Holding the circle with the twisted ends centered at the bottom,
collapse the circle in the middle until you have two ovals.

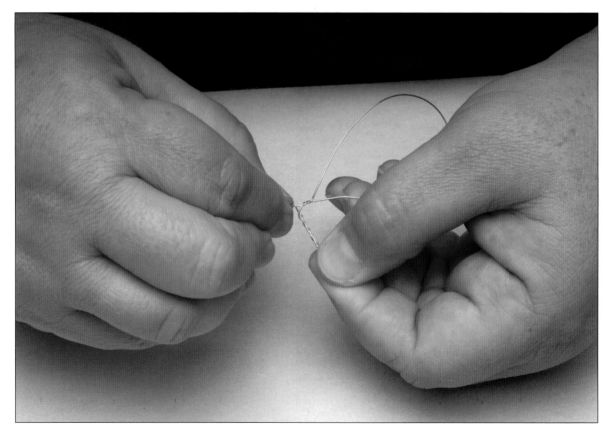

Twist the ovals two or three times to make wings.
Shape the wings as you like.

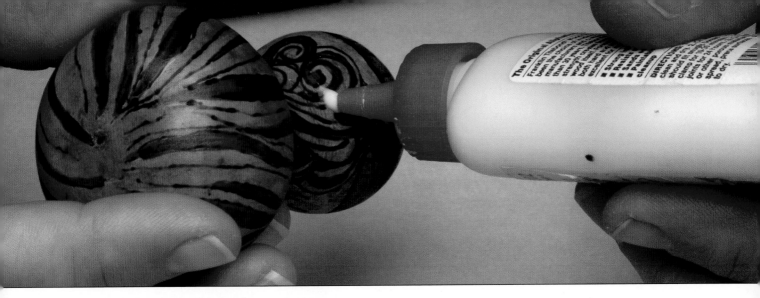

Using the fat darning needle, bore a hole into the upper back of the angel and squeeze wood glue into the hole.

Insert the twisted ends into the hole and bend the wings into position.

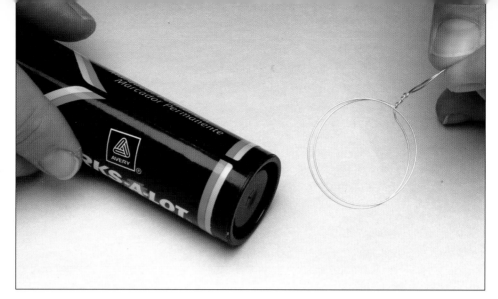

For the halo, cut enough wire to wrap around a grocery marker twice and twist the wire ends together four or five times. This twisted part will be the stem of the halo.

Bend the stem to be at the right angle to the halo.

Using a darning needle, bore a hole behind the center of the head for the stem of the halo. The halo should be positioned so it tilts back slightly from the face.

Squeeze wood glue into the hole and insert the stem into the hole.

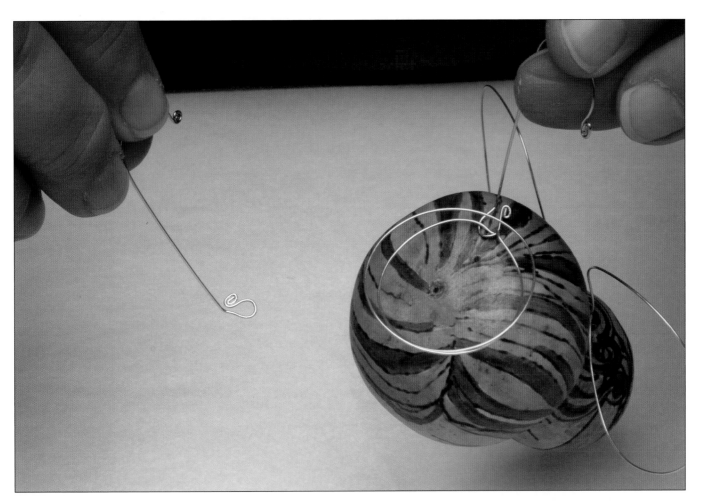

Once the wings and the halo holes have dried, suspend with an ornament hook, bending it to encircle the halo stem. Using gold thread tied to the halo stem would also work if you want the angel to twirl. The hook will be rigid.

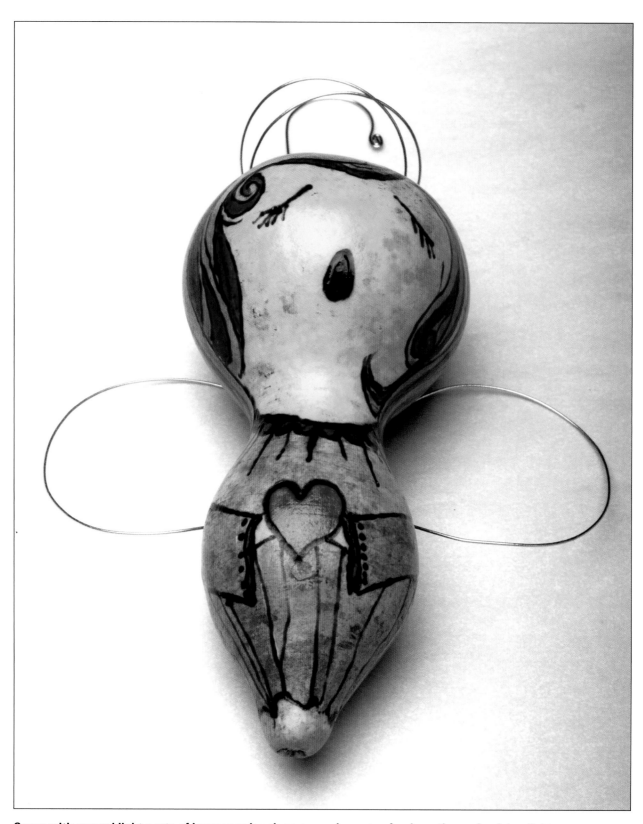

Spray with several light coats of lacquer or brush on a couple coats of polyurethane. Applying light coats will be the order of the day. There was a lot of marker ink used on this gourd and you do not want to risk a bleed if the lacquer coat is too thick.

Tree Ball and Double Tree Ball

The easiest way to get some gourd flash on the Christmas tree is to spray-paint several miniature gourds with shiny, metallic paint. Screw in some eyehooks, maybe add some beads or some glued-on plastic gems, and you are done. It's that easy! They show up well on green trees and, within an hour or two, you are on to the holiday baking. (In fact, truth be told, metallic paint will hide a whole host of flaws so you can use up some lesser quality gourds with dark spots that could not be used for other kinds of ornaments.)

Here are some ideas for a more elaborate ball:

Select a miniature gourd that is mostly circular, has a small top, and is free from flaws.

Here are some gourds with dark spots. These painted gourds had dark spots on them; one even had a bug hole that I filled with wood glue. Fast, highly effective.

Using a woodburner with a chisel tip, burn a wavy line around the belly of the circular gourd.

Continue the line around the belly until it meets where it began.

Color the interior spaces of the waves with permanent markers. You can consider using metallic permanent markers to add a bit of zip, but it is challenging to keep metallic marker ink from running into the burnt lines and looking messy.

Do a second, third, and fourth set of wavy lines that connect with the lines burned previously. This will look like waves of black lines meeting and pulling away from each other.

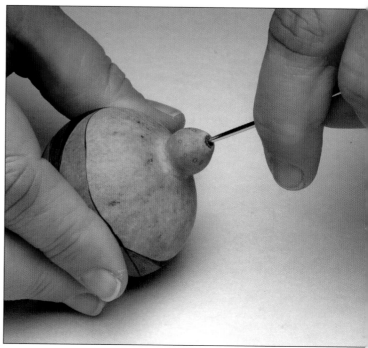

Bore a hole into the top of the gourd where the stem was.

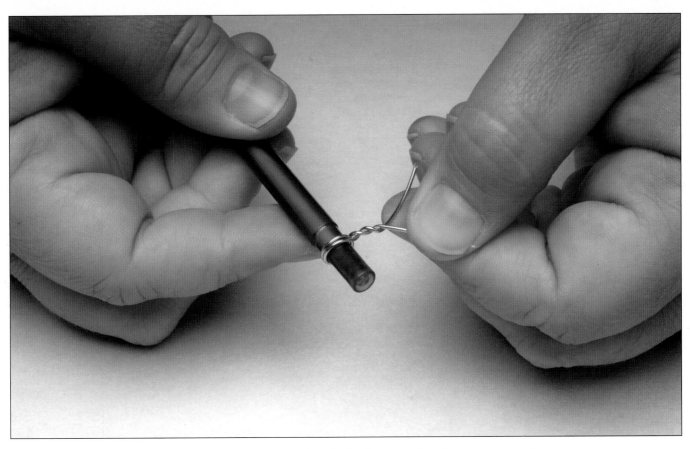

Cut a 3-4" piece of wire and make a Double Loop hanging device by wrapping the center around a pencil twice, forming a wire circle and giving the ends a twist.

Squeeze wood glue into the hole and insert the long ends of the wire circle into the hole and push the wire circle down toward the hole so it nestles in the space where the stem once grew.

After the glue has dried, suspend the ornament and spray lightly with a couple coats of lacquer or brush on a couple coats of polyurethane; allow time for drying between coats.

To make a Double Ball ornament, I will use two plain gourds for demonstration purposes.

Hold the bottom of each gourd at a right angle to a piece of sandpaper taped to a tabletop. Rub it against the sandpaper to create a flat area. Belt sanders work wonders if you're making dozens of these, but be careful not to sand away too much material.

Dot or spread wood glue on the flattened areas and bring them together. Let dry.

Follow the earlier directions for attaching a hanging device and finishing.

I am sure you can see the possibilities!

Tree Topper or Wall Hanging

Sometimes gourds and their stems can inspire a last minute idea, as these did when I came across them in the garage. Toothpicks, or tiny wooden dowels if you have them on hand, add tremendous strength that belies the delicate appearance of this bulbous concoction.

Select five miniature bottleneck gourds with long stems, preferably curved.

Trim any straggles off the stems so the ends are tidy.

Arrange the gourds in a star shape with stems going in the same direction, either clockwise or counter clockwise. The gourds should be touching at the bottom inside of the star and the stem ends should be on the outside of the star.

Position the gourds onto pieces of rolled duct tape so they are stable enough to mark for holes.

Touch the tip of a darning needle into a smidgeon of black craft paint. Slide the tip of the darning needle between the place where two gourds meet and will be connected.

Continue marking the meeting places all around.

Once all the connecting places are marked, use the darning needle to make a hole at the places where black marks the spot on each gourd.

Do this gourd by gourd, careful to replace each one to its original position as you go.

Cut five toothpicks in half.

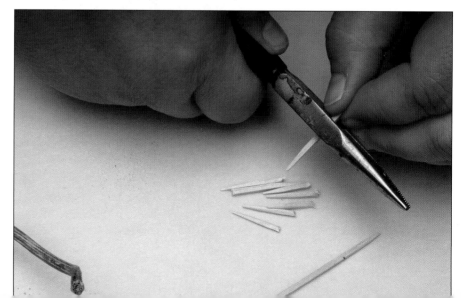

Squeeze wood glue into the holes where two gourds will connect.

Insert a toothpick into the side-by-side holes of the two gourds, and bring them together.

Continue this procedure around the star, connecting the gourds together. Make sure all gourds are snugly sitting next to each other. Let dry thoroughly.

Give the star a holiday shine by spraying it with a metallic paint.

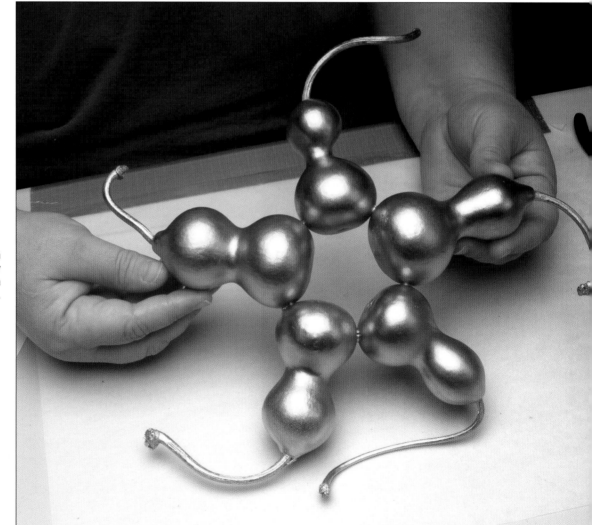

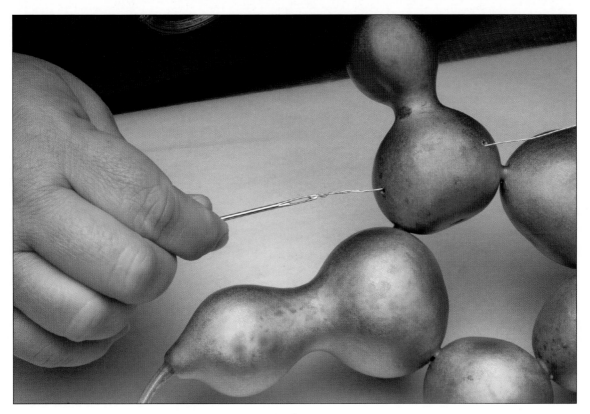

To tie the star to a tree: cut a foot or so of wire and, choosing the gourd at the top of the star, thread wire through the back of the bottom part of the gourd—the larger bulge.

Dab wood glue at the wire's entry and exit points to reinforce the holes. Let dry thoroughly.

Tie the star onto the top of the tree, or hang the star on a wall.

Part 3:

GALLERY

Here is a collection of the ornaments made in this book and some extras for inspiration. See how there are some snowmen different from what we made in our project pages? Inspiration for you to try new techniques on your own! They were made with a crackle finish paint I got at the hardware store. I use black wire wrapped around a pencil to make glasses, and a button on the belly.

Some of the plain gold-painted ornaments were dotted with glitter glue.

Some ornaments have a simple beaded ribbon glued on them.

Nothing was particularly pricey to make, but all have been satisfying.

Happy Gourding!

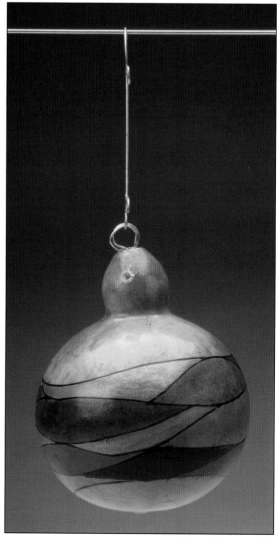